Beautiful Rollercoaster

Nickie LoVerde

BookLeaf
Publishing
India | USA | UK

Presentation by *BookLeaf Publishing*

Web: www.bookleafpub.com

E-mail: info@bookleafpub.com

ISBN: 9789357444552

First edition 2022

PREFACE

Life is so unexpected. It's a beautiful rollercoaster with twists and turns, ups and downs, with a perfect mix of thrills and fear. There is no rhyme or reason to the collection of poems enclosed. Some are connected to one another like the roots of a tree and others are complete strangers, not even sparing a passing glance to one another. Like each of us, each poem came to be at their own time and in their own way.

91821

I'm drowning
The drops fall relentlessly
I'm digging in to feel a different sort of pain
Anything to make it stop
The drops fall relentlessly

I'm mourning someone that never existed
My person, my confidant
The very best parts of me
Was never even there
I'm drowning

A beautiful facade
It was all in my head
What a beautiful imagination
Every smile, every knowing look
The very best parts
The drops fall relentlessly

I'm drowning
You're who I reach for when I can't breathe
But you aren't really there
Imaginary
I can't breathe
The drops fall relentlessly

Bluebird

A bluebird crossed my path today
My path yet still unclear
Unclear as a sky full of milky clouds
Clouds that whisper yet I still can't hear

A bluebird crossed my path today
Today as if to say to me, "Girl,"
"Girl, have you forgotten your heart?"
My heart beat faster still

A bluebird crossed my path today
A crossing on day three
Three days of greetings
Or perhaps misleadings, as she said to me,
"Why aren't you listening?"

A bluebird crossed my path today
Today, day four, tell me something more
"Something more or something true?"
"As true as your wings are blue"

A Book and a Houseplant

I stare at you from my proper place
I watch your tendrils grow
While I remain unchanged

Since you came into my world
You've far more attention than I
I am but a holder, of my proper place
You light up with the sunlight
While I fear it will affect me poorly
From white to yellow

Yellow we both fear
I wish I could protect you from here
My proper place

Though my story goes much further
To watch you continually grow
I am now that which is green

Tainted

I don't know where to begin
How to begin

You shattered me unintentionally
Indirectly, you shattered me

A kernel became a bomb inside of me
Obliterating everything

Every shared side smile
Every knowing look
Everything is tainted

My peace, my breath
Forgetting for instant, a half smile
The instant is over
Trying not to cry

I don't know how to be me
Without you
Which now is tainted, too.

Tainted Still

"Sometimes," you said to me.
"I wish you were more selfish."
So do I my darling, So do I.
But I can't share my pain,
What if it taints you, too?

Who Are you?

"Do you know who you are?"
I'm not sure I can answer that.
I haven't finished growing yet.
I haven't completed my journey.

"Do you know who you are?
Or just who you want to be?"
Struggling to compare the two
I'm finding I am not me without you
Or not the me I want to be, anyway.

Who I want to be is strong.
She can stand up on her own,
She can sing what's in her heart; strong and
steady.
A warrior for those who need
Someone to take the sword until they're ready.

"But do you know who you are?
Or just who you want to be?"
I want to make you proud
With everything inside of me.

But will that person be me?

Night and Day

There is beauty in the daylight
And beauty in the night
The day can be bright with promise
But night yields subtle longing
One cannot exist without the other
Can one's beauty show if the other was gone?
Would darkness still hold a comforting reprieve?
Would the dawn of a new day still bring hope?

Magic

There is a magic here
How could there not be?
Everything has its place
Even the wind passing through the trees and
wildflowers
A caressing hello, a feather light touch

There is magic here
Deep, deep in the woods
Every creature has its place
I am but a humble visitor
Grazing of gentle fingers
The soft bite of the bark

Completely alone, but not at all lonely
A quiet peace settles in
Shadows, a soothing embrace

Battles

One foot in front of the other
One breath at a time
Living, trying, surviving
The hardest path to choose
The choice itself a weight
Every day a battle
Battles fought to win a war
A never ending struggle
To endure is to prevail
To live, to try, to survive is to win

Tick Tock

What do you want to do?
Who do you want to be?
Tick tock, tick tock

What brings you joy?
What makes you happy?
Tick tock, tick tock

Nothing is forever
Nothing is ever free
Tick tock, tick tock

"The greatest joy!"
"A love like no other!"
"A blessing! A miracle"
Tick tock, tick tock

You made it, you're safe
Stability...
Security...
Comfort...
But I'm sorry, time's up

Feel It

When you feel like your world is imploding
There is someone whose home is exploding
Perspective
Guilt
Encouraged to feel, but not too deeply now
"It can always be worse!"
But the burn won't relent
Feel it
Acknowledge it
Release it
You're still alive
Feel it
Embrace it
Live.

If It Makes You Happy

A belle of the ball
You smile and laugh with them all
Your eyes seek out mine as you place your hand
on his arm
Making sure I am watching as his head bows
toward yours
A whisper
I look away
The fire inside me burns
I'll take the fire any day
Over the nothing you must feel to act this way

Hello Again

Hello again Bluebird
I've been waiting for you
Had almost lost hope
Have you brought answers this time?
So many questions
I thought they would slow with time
But there are only more each day
Don't stray too far Bluebird

Home

Comfort, ease, relief
Eyes closed, deep breaths, lungs full
I thought I'd found you
Time is fleeting
Forever searching

Wild Flower

Against all odds
Beauty blooms
Blooms and thrives
Time passes
Life, not in spite of
But hand in hand, with death

More Questions

Birds keep flying
Fish keep swimming
Do they too face these trials?
Questioning everything
To fly, to swim, to march
Is there any direction?

Freya

I stroke my felines as we ride
We fly, and I search, and I weep
The clock in Valhalla will chime
Oh where, oh where can Odr be?

My tears they fall like amber rain
Upon the land, the trees, the sea
Within my cloak, conceal the pain
His tricks, his lies, Loki will surely best me

The elves, the dwarves, giants, and Gods
They beg, they plead, they worship beneath me
What good are men when most have claws
Yet my face still calm and filled with beauty

An act, a façade, until I find him
Whatever it takes, 'till we meet again

I Would Love You

I would miss you
Had you been mine to miss
I would mourn you
Had you been mine to mourn
I would have protected you
Had you been mine to fight for
I would have loved you

Lines

Black and white
Right and Wrong
The lines keep shifting,
as if swaying in the wind
At times they are sure, firm
Other times blurred
Bleary, like sunlight reaching through water
Seeking

Three

Sharp and strong
An unyielding bond
Forever three
Arrows to fly through time
Through distance
Through life
Where one falters
Two hold firm
When two falter
The third holds firm
Three points, three souls
Forever bound

Dark

Beginning, middle, end
Where does one stop and the next begin?
Are you strong enough to stand beside me?
Light, then dark, then darker still.